STAGE 1

BOOK 2

TATTOO

Philippa Bateman

RISING ★ **STARS**

Jack took off his hoodie.

Gran Val shook her finger at Jack.
She took off her coat.

CHECK

1. Was Jack's tattoo real?

2. Did Jack think he could fool Gran Val?

3. Why do you think Gran Val shook her finger at Jack?

FIND

Find the words to fill the gaps.

1. I've got a _____ .   (page 5)

2. Gran Val _____ her finger at Jack.   (page 12)

3. She took off her _____ .   (page 12)

What's missing?

1. check this out   (page 2)

2. she will be so mad with you   (page 8)

3. i got it from a comic book   (page 10)

*Put the **verbs** (took, fool, check) in the right gaps.*

1. _____ this out.   (page 2)

2. Jack _____ off his hoodie.   (page 7)

3. Let me see if I can _____ her too.   (page 11)

WORD POWER

Put it right.

1. out this Check.   (page 2)

2. real It's not.   (page 10)

3. I got it from a book comic.   (page 10)

Swap the word in **bold** *for a new word that means the opposite.*

4. She will be so **mad** with you!

5. Jack **took off** his hoodie.